ISBN 978-1-331-58494-0
PIBN 10209102

This book is a reproduction of an important historical work. Forgotten Books uses
state-of-the-art technology to digitally reconstruct the work, preserving the original format
whilst repairing imperfections present in the aged copy. In rare cases, an imperfection in
the original, such as a blemish or missing page, may be replicated in our edition. We do,
however, repair the vast majority of imperfections successfully; any imperfections that
remain are intentionally left to preserve the state of such historical works.

THE CERTAINTY OF DIVINE FAITH.

A SERMON

PREACHED ON THE

FEAST OF ST. THOMAS THE APOSTLE, 1853,

IN THE

CHURCH OF ST. GREGORY THE GREAT, IN ROME,

At the Solemn Benediction

OF THE

RIGHT REVEREND FATHER M. BERNARD BURDER,

BY

HENRY EDWARD MANNING, D.D.

LONDON:

BURNS AND LAMBERT, 17 PORTMAN STREET,

PORTMAN SQUARE.

1854.

Any proceeds which may arise from the sale of this S will be at the disposal of the F. Abbot.

TO

THE RIGHT REVEREND THE ABBOT

OF

THE CISTERTIAN MONASTERY OF ST. BERNARD'S,

IN CHARNWOOD FOREST,

WHO,

IN TOKEN OF THE FAITH WHICH THOUGH MARTYRED CAN NEVER DIE,

BUT THROUGH SUFFERING EVER RENEWS ITS STRENGTH,

RECEIVED SOLEMN BENEDICTION

AT THE HANDS OF THE SUCCESSOR OF ST. AUGUSTINE,

APOSTLE OF ENGLAND,

ON THE CŒLIAN HILL,

FROM WHENCE CAME FORTH THE EVANGELISTS AND PASTORS

OF THE ANGLO-SAXON RACE,

This Sermon

IS AFFECTIONATELY INSCRIBED.

CERTAINTY OF DIVINE FAITH.

" Thomas answered and said to Him : My Lord and my God.
Jesus saith to him : Because thou hast seen me, Thomas,
thou hast believed : blessed are they that have not seen, and
have believed."—St. John xx. 28, 29.

It was not by chance, brethren, as the Church
teaches us by the words of St. Gregory, read in
the matins of this festival, that St. Thomas was
not with the other Disciples when Jesus came.
His Divine Master permitted him for a time to
doubt, as He also permitted Lazarus, whom He
loved, to die, of whom He said, " This sickness
is not unto death, but for the glory of God ; that
the Son of Man may be glorified by it."   In the
unbelief of Thomas there were, as we now see,
deep purposes of grace both to him and to us.

The notices we have of St. Thomas in Holy
Scripture are few ; and yet, though few, they are
full of meaning.   They set before us, as by the
master-strokes of a divine hand, the whole out-
line of his character.   The first three Evangelists record his name alone in the number of the

twelve Apostles. St. John only three times has recorded his words: once, when Jesus would go into Judea again, where the Jews had lately sought to kill Him, St. Thomas broke forth with vehement devotion, "Let us also go, that we may die with Him."* And again, when our Lord, preparing for His departure, had said, "Whither I go, you know, and the way you know," Thomas took up His words, with the impatience of love and sorrow, "Lord, we know not whither Thou goest, and how can we know the way?"† And once more, when the other Disciples said unto him, "We have seen the Lord," the same resolute heart broke forth, "Except I shall see in His hand the print of the nails, and put my finger into the place of the nails, and put my hand into His side, I will not believe."‡ And for this unbelief he met a divine rebuke: "Because thou hast seen Me, thou hast believed." In what, then, was the unbelief of Thomas more to be blamed than the unbelief of all the rest? When the women came, saying that He was risen, the Disciples thought it to be "idle tales;" of both Peter and John—Peter, who by revelation of the Father had already confessed that Jesus was the Christ, the Son of God; John, who lay upon His bosom at supper — even of

---

* St. John xi. 4.   ‡ St. John xx. 25.

† St. John xiv. 4, 5.

these chiefest Apostles we read that they ran to the sepulchre, and "believed;" that is, believed that He was not there, as the women had told them; for "as yet" they knew not the Scripture, "that He must rise again from the dead."* Of all the Disciples, too, we know that He appeared to them "as they were at table, and upbraided them with their incredulity and hardness of heart, because they did not believe them who had seen Him after He was risen again."† And when at last He came to them, "they yet believed not, and wondered for joy."‡ Where, then, was the special fault of Thomas? It was in the stubbornness and wilfulness of his heart, which not only refused to believe, but prescribed the evidence without which he would not be persuaded. The fault lay deep in the secret springs of the will, seen by the Searcher of hearts alone.

And after eight days of doubting, hope, and fear, His Disciples were again within, and Thomas with them. Then came Jesus, and stood in the midst; the air of a sudden seemed to give up His form visible to their sight, and He said, "Peace be to you." Then at once, with divine intuition, He said to Thomas, "Put in thy finger hither, and see My hands; and bring hither thy hand, and put it into My side, and be not faith-

* St. John xx. 9.   ‡ St. Luke xxiv. 41.
† St. Mark xvi. 14.

less, but believing. Thomas answered and said to Him, My Lord and my God. Jesus saith to him, Because thou hast seen Me, Thomas, thou hast believed: blessed are they that have not seen, and have believed." See here the tenderness and condescension of the Son of God for the sake of one soul; and to heal the unbelief of one soul He gave the very proof prescribed, He manifested the wounds of His Divine Manhood. How light and gentle fell His upbraiding on the faithless Disciple! It is only not a benediction; the words of reproof, almost before they are fully heard, pass into a blessing: " Blessed are they that have not seen, and have believed."

Most needful and wholesome are such words in these latter days, when it is towards evening, and the light of truth casts long shadows on the earth. The times seem now to be at hand which our Lord foretold: " But yet the Son of Man when He cometh, shall He find, think you, faith on earth?"* Truly the days of doubt are come; for men spend their lives in objecting, disputing, and refusing to believe. They censure St. Thomas, yet outstrip him in incredulity. Truths which transcend the reason are to them incredible; as if the mysteries of God were not as far above the reason of man as the revolutions of the heavens above our petty movements upon earth. The same people

* St. Luke xviii. 8.

who profess to believe the miracles of the Apostles disbelieve the miracles of Saints; and yet the
same temper which makes them faithless in the
presence of Almighty power at this day, would
have made them equally unbelieving then. They
who appeal from the miracles of Saints to the miracles of the Apostles would then have appealed from
the miracles of Apostles to the miracles of Elisha.
So, again, there are those who profess to believe
the divine power and commission of the Apostles,
but refuse to believe the divine mission and power
of the Church; and yet, in the days of the Apostles, they would have equally appealed from them
to the authority of Moses. The reason is all one;
the true cause is, that they will not believe in the
presence and power of Jesus here and now, work-
ing among us as at the beginning. They are cold,
and slow of heart; they criticise and object; they
prescribe the kind and the quantity of proof without which they will not believe. "Except I shall
see in His hands the print of the nails," and "I
will not believe." This cold temper finds its way
even among the faithful; for there are those who
hanker after the sensible and lower manifestation
of the presence of Jesus; they excuse their feeble
and dim faith by saying: "If I had lived in the
days when He was upon earth; if I could but
have seen the majesty of His form and the beauty
of His countenance; if I could but have heard

the accent of His voice and the sweetness of His words,—I should believe with a faith all vivid and fervent, and persevere without relaxation to the end."

But what, after all, is this too, but to assume that the dispensation under which they were who saw Him in the flesh was a dispensation heavenly and divine, and that the state in which we are now is human and earthly; that in those days God manifested Himself by explicit works and signs of power which now are passed away; that we are at a disadvantage, and have fainter proofs, fewer helps, and greater hindrances to faith? This is but another form of the general unbelief of these latter times.

The reverse is the truth. They were in the beginning, we in the fulness of the kingdom of God; they were in the dawn, and we in the splendour of the day. The dispensations of faith, from just Abel until the last Saint on earth, is but one and continuous; it has had many stages and periods of expansion, unfolding from light to light, from grace to grace; but Patriarchs, Prophets, and Saints of old did not receive the fulness of the promises, God having reserved " some better thing for us, that they should not be perfected without us."* We have received what they foretold and saw not; for " God who at sundry times and in

* Heb. xi. 40.

divers manners spoke in times past to the Fathers by the Prophets, last of all in these days hath spoken to us by His Son."* And yet even in this last crowning revelation of His kingdom, there are stages and periods of advance. It began in the moment of the Incarnation; but it had its fulness when the Incarnate Son ascended into heaven, and sent down the Holy Ghost upon His Church. We, then, lack nothing that they enjoyed; we have all, and more; they had but the fore running lights of the morning, we have the dayspring and the noontide of grace and truth.·

The fulness of the kingdom of Faith, which we have received, consists of three divine gifts, greater than all ever bestowed before upon mankind.

First: We have, for the foundation of our faith, an infallible testimony. If they had certainty, we have even more. We have their own testimony, the certainty of those who saw and spake with the Lord Jesus after He rose from the dead. Their testimony is not passed away, but is now living, fresh and stedfast. We have the testimony of Mary and the women who were with her, of Cleophas and of his fellow; of the Disciples who believed, and of Thomas who doubted. His doubting, as St. Gregory teaches, avails us more than their belief. It is a double certainty, and a countersign of their witness. We have, moreover,

* Heb. i. 1.

not their faith alone, but the witness of all nations who by the word of the Apostles believed in the kingdom of Jesus Christ. The whole earth, from the rising to the setting of the sun, became one world-wide testimony to the advent of the Word made flesh. It was a supernatural expansion of the attestation of the chosen witnesses who saw Him in the forty days before He ascended to His Father's throne. The whole earth responded to the message of God, and became as it were the eye-witness and ear-witness of the resurrection of Jesus. And yet more, we have not only the testimony of all nations at that day, but of all ages, from the morning when He rose again until this hour. The universal voice of Christendom, from generation to generation, has handed on this supernatural fact, with an evidence which expands and multiplies itself as time runs on. Every martyrdom is a seal set to the word of Jesus; every act of faith, of hope, of charity, all the energies and achievements of confessors, the deeds and patience of saints in every age,—are so many attestations and signatures upon the great record of truth. And God makes even the unwilling to serve Him; for the whole weight of human history, like the soldiers who kept the sepulchre, adds its testimony to the faith of the Church of God. And yet people object, and say that they saw our Lord, but we only hear; that they had the evidence of

their very senses, we have never seen nor heard
Him. What is this, at last, but a low and ani-
mal philosophy? Sense is not our surest instru-
ment of knowledge. Nay, it is the lowest, the
narrowest, and in some matters the most easily
deceived. For what is sense but the medium
through which we converse with this visible and
lower world; with its phenomena, its motions,
operations, and changes? The sphere and ken of
sense is scanty and limited; it reaches only to the
outer surface, under which all is to sense unknown.
Sense needs the reason to be its interpreter and
guide; for, with all its confidence, sense is blind.
Without the higher light of reason, the laws, principles, causes, and conditions of all it sees, handles,
and knows, are unknown. And yet the reason in
its sphere is bounded too. A world of intellectual
objects, the phenomena of a higher, but not the
highest sphere, are within its ken. The Unseen
and the Eternal are beyond its gaze; and of these,
except by another faculty higher than sense or
reason, supernatural in its substance and its acts,
which comes to perfect both, we know nothing.
It is not by sense nor by reason, but by faith,
elevating both, that the truths of the kingdom of
·God are known and believed. We read this in
every page of the gospels. The Jews went by
sense.. They saw Jesus, and believed Him to be a
man like themselves: " Is not this Jesus ·the son

of Joseph, whose father and mother we know? how then saith he, I came down from heaven?"* Nicodemus added reason to sense, and perceived that the mission and person of Jesus were divine: "We know that Thou art a teacher come from God; for no man can do these signs which Thou doest except God be with him."† But he could ascend no further; reason had touched its bound. Peter could say, "Thou art Christ, the Son of the living God;"‡ because flesh and blood had not revealed it unto him; neither human sense nor natural reason, but the Father which is in heaven. It was by faith that he saw, knew, and confessed the Godhead and Sonship of his Master. So with those who saw Him after He rose from the dead; they saw not the true and divine object of their faith. Thomas, as St. Gregory says, saw His manhood, and confessed His Godhead. The testimony of sense was but the motive to believe, the footing from which he rose upward by faith to truth. So it is now with us. What the visible manhood and presence of Jesus was to Thomas, the visible form of His mystical body manifest upon earth is to us. We, too, see His presence visible in the Church, and confess and adore His Godhead. This is the true and formal object of our faith, which is surer than all sense, higher

* St. John vi. 42.   ‡ St. Matt. xvi. 16.
† St. John iii. 2.

than all reason, perfecting both. Faith has a certainty of its own above all other kinds; above the certainty of science, different in its nature, loftier in its reach, deeper in its conviction; for it unites the reason of man with God, the eternal, changeless truth.

But again : we have not only an outer testimony, we have an inward witness beyond all ever bestowed on man before the day of Pentecost,—the full illumination of the kingdom of God. Before the ascension of our Divine Lord, we read that even Apostles knew not the Scriptures. Cleophas and his fellow " hoped that it was He that should have redeemed Israel;"* and the eleven, at the hour of His ascension, asked, " Lord, wilt Thou at this time restore again the kingdom to Israel ?"† They knew Christ after the flesh, and their faith was not yet unfolded. Therefore our Lord said to them, " It is expedient to you that I go;"‡ for you the withdrawal of My visible Presence is needful. " For if I go not, the Paraclete will not come to you; but if I go, I will send Him to you; and when He is come, He will teach you all things, and bring all things to your mind."§ " The spirit of truth shall be with you and in you" for ever. And on the day of Pentecost the Holy Ghost fell upon them, and His illumination

* St. Luke xxiv. 21.   ‡ St. John xvi. 7.
† Acts i. 6.   § St. John xiv. 26.

filled their inmost soul; their whole intelligence was enlightened, a fountain of light sprang up from within, and truths already known were unfolded with new and deeper meanings. They saw the full mystery of the kingdom of God, of the Father, of the Son, and of the Holy Ghost; of the love of the Father in the gift of His Son, of the Son in giving Himself to be made man to suffer and to die; of the Holy Ghost, who was already upon them and within them. They perceived that their Divine Master had ascended to sit down upon His Father's throne, crowned with power to possess His kingdom; and the whole earth to them was lightened with His glory. " The true light which enlighteneth every man that cometh into this world,"* was revealed. A greater light from above fell upon the lesser light of nature, and the ciphers and characters of truth inscribed upon this visible world were interpreted with an unknown and divine meaning. The witness of creation ascended into a full revelation of the glory and the Godhead of the Blessed Three, the Holy One, Eternal; and this light is stedfast and changeless until now. It fills the whole world. It ante-dates all argument. It proposes the revelation of God to all who are within the name and sphere of Christendom.

* St. John i. 9.

The knowledge of God in Christ has taken its place among the immediate perceptions of our intelligence. It comes to us before we seek it. We have the conclusion before the reasons; and our intellectual acts are but as a logical analysis and ordering of the proofs which both in nature and in grace God has given us of Himself. From the earliest use of reason even the unbeliever and the sceptic receive a knowledge of God and of His law, which, without revelation, he could never obtain. By his own argument, or out of his own consciousness, he could never elicit it. With the light of revelation he despises revelation; and is the subject of it whether he will or no. So, too, the heretic, and they who will believe only fragments of truth; all the light they have, in which to criticise and weigh and pronounce upon the doctrines of the faith, they derive involuntarily and unconsciously from the illumination in which they are encompassed. In faithful hearts, this effusion of light generates the spiritual consciousness of things unseen and divine which springs up with faith. The whole intelligence is elevated to the supernatural order, in which the mysteries of the kingdom of God are principles, axioms, truths, self-evident and manifest in their own immediate light; "for God who commanded the light to shine out of darkness, hath shined in our hearts, to give the light of the knowledge of the glory of God in the face of Jesus Christ."*

But once more: we have received not only a witness in the reason, but a testimony in the heart. When our Lord had ascended up on high, He shed abroad the gift of the Holy Ghost, the uncreated charity of God into our hearts. As He promised in Jerusalem, "If any man thirst, let him come to Me and drink." "He that believeth in Me, as the Scripture saith, out of his belly shall flow rivers of living water. Now this He said (writes the Evangelist) of the Spirit, which they should receive who believed in Him; for as yet the Spirit was not given, because Jesus was not yet glorified."† When, on the day of Pentecost, the Holy Ghost descended, He came not only as a light to illuminate the intelligence, but as charity, both to kindle the heart and to inspire the will. The whole inward nature was then elevated by the immediate operation of Supernatural Grace. The witness of faith is countersigned by a testimony within. "The Spirit Himself giveth testimony to our spirit that we are the sons of God."‡ "He that believeth in the Son of God hath the testimony of God in himself."§ And this Divine gift of uncreated charity, by which the

* 2 Cor. iv. 6.　　　　　　‡ Rom. viii. 16.
† St. John vii. 37-39.　　　§ 1 St. John v. 10.

faithful are made perfect, has descended through the Church unto this hour. We know Him, by an inward perception of the heart, to be our kinsman in the supernatural consanguinity of the Incarnation, our Brother by participation of flesh and blood, our Lord Incarnate and our God. "Blessed are they who have not seen, and have believed;" who live amidst the Divine manifestations of the Word made flesh; blessed, because sight and sense no longer prompt their faith, but a prompt readiness to believe, which springs from a loving heart, and a will conformed to the will of God. Blessed, because any act of faith springing from a free and fervent will merits, in the sight of our Heavenly Father, according to the measure in which it is generous and confiding. It draws down from Him larger infusions of His graces, and shall win a brighter crown and a more abundant measure of reward in the kingdom of eternal life. If such is our state, what hinders faith in us? Nothing on God's part; He has done all for us, and more than for those whose names of old were in the roll of the faithful. Truth and Grace, both without us and within, are abundantly vouchsafed. Where, then, is the hindrance? Not on the part of our intelligence, which has motives and testimonies sufficient beyond measure to awaken and to generate faith. Where, then, can the hindrance be found, but where it was in Thomas, in the will: "I will not believe." There is some bribe which makes us partial, some end out of sight, some hope, or fear, or pledge, lying as it were under the horizon, which, like a loadstone, makes us untrue to truth and to ourselves. Though truth were resplendent as the sun in heaven, yet it is as a sackcloth of hair to those who will not see. I do not now speak of the more gross and poisonous sins, which deaden the inward sight, and dull the ear of the heart, but of more refined and subtle sins of the spirit and of the will. Love of the world, a craving after honour, fear of man, the influence of a position, or social relations; over-attachment to home and friends; self-trust, self-will, a spirit of criticism on that deepest of mysteries; a warp in the will itself, of which no human eye can find the cause,—all these will hinder faith, even in the full light of truth. As our Lord has said, "How can you believe, who receive glory one from another; and the glory which is from God alone you do not seek?" And to the young man, whom when He saw He loved, Jesus said: "One thing is wanting unto thee. Go, sell whatsoever thou hast, and give to the poor, and thou shalt have treasure in heaven, and come, follow Me: who, being struck sad at that saying, went away sorrowful, for he had great possessions."* If,

* St. Mark x. 21, 22.

then, we would believe with Thomas, we must overcome and cast out self; for " with the heart we believe unto justice."

There are two things that God loves, simplicity and sincerity. Simplicity, which has no double or fold, but is open and truthful; sincerity, which has no mixture of self and second thoughts, but is clear and transparent as the light. " The light of thy body is thy eye; if thy eye be single, thy whole body shall be lightsome; if thy eye be evil, thy whole body shall be darksome; if, then, the light that is in thee be darkness, the darkness itself how great shall it be !"* Again, if we would cast out self, we must correspond with the grace we have already received. God waits for the will of man; not the natural will, which is impotent to elicit supernatural acts, but for the will already elevated by grace to the power of corresponding with the will of God. " Behold, I stand at the gate and knock : if any man shall hear My voice, and open to Me, I will come in to him, and sup with him, and he with Me."† And, as the Church in Council has said : " Not a moment passes but God stands at the gate, and knocks." The whole life of faith is a chain of these deliberate acts; each one of which is done by the power of grace; and as grace is used, it is by the mercy and gift of God perpetually increased, until the whole heart

* St. Matt. vi. 22, 23.   † Apoc. iii. 20.

is cleared of self, and filled only with the presence and mind of Christ. What greatness and what grandeur of soul in those who live no more unto themselves, but in and to Christ alone; how vast in aim, how fruitful in works, how enduring in perseverance! When Christ is formed in the heart, and faith is made perfect in charity, the whole soul is His to live and to die. Do we ask for an example of such faith to-day? We need not go far to find it. Here, on this very spot, was one whose whole life and its achievements bear witness to the power of faith. In this, the home of his patrician forefathers, though young in years yet ripe in heart, he lived in honour and splendour, invested with the highest civic dignities; he sat chief in the capitol and the basilica, and walked abroad with the insignia of rule through the city and the forum. But the heart of Gregory was weaned within him from all earthly pomp; he had seen by 'faith the glory of the eternal world; and this had lost its brightness. By one act of faith all was laid aside for Christ, and his palace became the house of religious brethren. All around us are the tokens of his memory; the chamber where he rested, the chair in which he taught; and here, under the oaks which shadowed the Cœlian hill, he meditated upon eternity and God. Another voice than mine, still fresh in your memories, has told you what it was

that wakened in his heart the desire to win to
Christ an island on the outskirts of the world,
deep in the northern seas. As he mused, the fire
which Jesus came to send upon the earth kindled
within him. He offered himself to bear the word
of life to the Saxon people. His sacrifice, like
that of the Patriarch of old, was accepted. For
three days he journeyed forth a wayfarer towards
Britain; when his self-oblation was complete, the
hand of God turned him back again to Rome.
Gregory was not chosen to be the apostle; the
time of grace for England was not yet come.
Long years were yet to pass; he was to be forced
from his haven of peace, immersed in public cares;
wafted beyond the Adriatic, long to dwell in the
imperial city on the shores of the Bosphorus.
Long years again were yet to run ere he should
return to the peace of his home upon the Cœlian.
At last Gregory ruled the Church of God, and the
time for the long-sown seed to spring was come.
Then, from this very hill, went forth Augustine
with the companions of his glorious embassy.
You need not, brethren, that I recount what all
know so well. Beautiful upon the white shores
of Britain were the feet of those that preached the
glad tidings of the heavenly kingdom. Beautiful
upon the bleak eastern coast of Thanet was the
long array, as an army with banners, which with
solemn chant followed the silver cross and the

pictured form of the Son of God into the presence
of the King of Kent. But Ethelbert and Bertha,
and Thanet and Canterbury, are familiar names.
The work of Gregory in England was begun; its
growth was rapid, and its fruitfulness divine.
Ages flew past, and Bishops ruled in Canterbury
and Rochester, and London and York, and Lin-
coln and Lichfield, and Dorchester and Selsey;
names dear to memory, though the Church of
God knows them now no more. And from Glas-
tonbury and Southwell, and Ripon and Hexham,
and Westminster, matins and vespers ascended
morning and evening before the eternal throne.
The kingdoms of Kent, and Mercia, and North-
umberland, the Saxons of the east and of the
west, and of the south, ever in warfare until now,
laid down their weapons, and came into the kingdom of God. The kings of the seven people
brought their honour and glory into the city of
the Lamb. The history of England, Saxon and
Catholic, as it comes down to us in the pages of
St. Bede, is like a tradition of Paradise. And yet
he wrote of it, not as we see it now, through the
dimness and softness of ages, but living before
his eyes. For sweetness, saintliness, and beauty
not of this earth, there is nothing nobler or more
touching in the annals of the Church of God. In
union with the universal kingdom of Christ, and
under the rule of the See of Peter, England was

encompassed with the Communion of Saints; and the very course of nature seemed to be supernatural.

For kings it had saints. St. Oswald and St. Oswin, St. Edward and St. Edmund, are numbered among the martyrs; St. Edwin and St. Edward among confessors, and of its royal blood many more beside. Among its pastors, St. Swithin, St. Erconwald, St. Elphege, St. Wilfred, St. Chad, and a roll too many to be named, are among the Saints of God. The very soil was consecrated by names and by memories sweet and imperishable. They are upon it to this day, the household words of England. Such was the work of Gregory, as yet in its freshness and its childhood. It had a manhood yet to come; an age rude and mighty, a time of monarchy and splendour, of higher civilisation and riper culture; when the Normans ruled in England, and its prelates, its princes, its statesmen, and its doctors, were in renown through the courts and universities of Europe. But saints waxed few, and the martyrs and confessors of England, St. Anselm and St. Thomas, St. Edmund, and St. Richard, won their crowns in conflict with princes who ruled from the thrones of St. Edmund and St. Edward. The times were already out of course, and for ages there might be seen growing up the causes of some fatal struggle. At last it came. Out broke the great revolt; a

time of which I need say little now.   It is vividly
before the minds of all.   The spirit of faith had
departed, and the spirit of doubt, with twelve
legions of his angels, entered in; then came forth
once more martyrs and confessors as in days of
old.   The bishops of the flock were thrust rudely
from their thrones.   God's priests were exiled,
hunted down and slain; the flock driven or misled
into strange pastures.   Faith was turned into the
jangling of controversy, and the sweet and solemn
ritual was marred and dishonoured.   The light
before the tabernacle was put out, and the tabernacle rudely tumbled from the altar; the altar,
stone by stone, was broken down.   And all this
because the Real Presence had departed; while
the disputer and the doubter kept on their loud
debate: "Except I shall see in His hands the
print of the nails, and put my finger into the
place of the nails, I will not believe."   Truly, it
has come to pass, for with faith in the Sacramen-
tal Presence of the Word made flesh has well nigh
departed also faith in the Incarnation of the
Eternal Son.   Many deny it; still more live as if
they believed it not; and even to those who profess
it, a cold dim haze hangs between them and the
divine Manhood and the sacred Heart of Jesus.
England was lost to the Church of God.

Is then the work of Gregory come to nought?
And has the malice of man prevailed against it?

No, it has not perished. I shall seem, perhaps, to speak at random if I say it is greater now than ever. Yet it is the very truth. Gregory's work is vaster, and more widely spread, than in all ages past. It was not without design that when England revolted from the faith, Ireland and Scotland made its speech their own. They have again entered, as of old, to restore the faith of England, and to mingle with its people. God in His inscrutable wisdom has twice replenished our land by faithful of another race. The Catholic Church of Britain and of the British Empire preaches the word of life throughout the world. The world is full of its missions; the Saxon people for two centuries have been in perpetual migration throughout the earth. They have peopled Northern America along both its coasts; they are in its boundless centre; the shores of India, the islands of the west and of the south are their home. St. Gregory at this hour has more sons in faith than peopled all England before it revolted from the Holy See; the hierarchy of St. Augustine has reproduced itself fivefold beyond the number of sees which the schism rent away. The dispersion of the English race, like the scattering of the Greek and of the Roman in old time, is beyond doubt a prelude of some mightier movement in the earth than the world as yet has seen. What may be hereafter we know not; for the future who can tell?

Prophecy is not ours, but work and faith. And yet we may discern the signs of the earth and of the sky. And all point to one expectation, to some vaster sway of empire than any known to history. Who cannot see, at least, the outlines of the future in the tide of civilisation which is now setting in full stream towards Central America, where the Mississippi pours its mighty waters through valleys boundless in vastness and fertility, washing the walls of cities which may one day be the capitals of the West. Under the southern stars, in the continent of Australia, the foundations of a power are being laid which may one day rule the East. Who can foresee into how many kingdoms and empires the colonies of England and the States of America, as ripe seeds cast from the parent tree, may hereafter spring? And already the Catholic Church has measured these vast foundations, and laid the corner-stones of an hierarchy which shall embrace the world. Already, too, the sons of St. Ignatius and St. Alphonsus, the sons and daughters of St. Vincent, and others without number of every spiritual family in the Church, are pushing onward in their provident charity even beyond the bounds of civilisation. America will not refuse St. Augustine as its apostle, or St. Gregory as its patriarch in the kingdom of God. Whence sprung this world-wide mission of Anglo-Saxon faith, but from the fervent heart which mused upon the Cœlian Mount? It was even here that the soul of Gregory, emptied of self, and full only of the mind of Jesus, conceived the purpose which has borne so mighty a growth.

It is good for us to be here. We are met around the fountains of our faith. The Saxons of the slave-market are become the people of God. They are here this day to continue the work which St. Gregory began. The primate of the Anglo-Saxon Church is here. The true successor and the rightful heir of St. Augustine's pall. And he is here to bless a spiritual head and father over one among the families sprung from the lineage of St. Benedict. Into his hands has been delivered the rule, the same in its letter as some contend, the very same in its substance as all know, with the rule which Gregory obeyed in this sacred place. Around the primate of the Church in England are here gathered a number of its priesthood and of its faithful; and a band of young ardent spirits sprung from Saxon blood, who are here to kindle their manly zeal at the ashes of the Apostles, and to form their high resolves where Gregory sacrificed, and the names of Augustine, Mellitus, and Justus speak from the cloister-wall. Gregory is still living and giving life. Twelve centuries have passed, but the work of faith is here. Saxon England is passed, and Norman England is no more. The monarchy of France has changed and vanished; the empires of the east and of the west have gone their way; the powers of Europe have been moulded and remoulded once and again; but the Church of God stands firm, the same yesterday, to-day, and for ever; the symbol and partaker of the immutability of its Divine Head. O imperishable Church of God! on whom time falls light, over whom man has no power; whence is this undying life? On thy part it is the presence of the Incarnate Word; on ours it is a faith that knows no doubt. This is what England needs; not wealth, not intellect, not power (though all be good because gifts of God), but the supernatural grace of faith. Purify our hearts, pluck up every root and fibre of self, and fill us with Thine own unchanging Presence. Lord, we ask not to see the print of the nails. We have Thy five Sacred Wounds, through which, hour by hour, all grace descends from the Eternal Father; through which all our prayers and hopes ascend to Him again. We ask not to put our hand into Thy side. We have Thy Sacred Heart, Thy love divine in the sympathies of our manhood, ever open to us, the object of our worship, the pattern of our life, the fountain of all grace. We believe; for Thou art our Lord and our God.

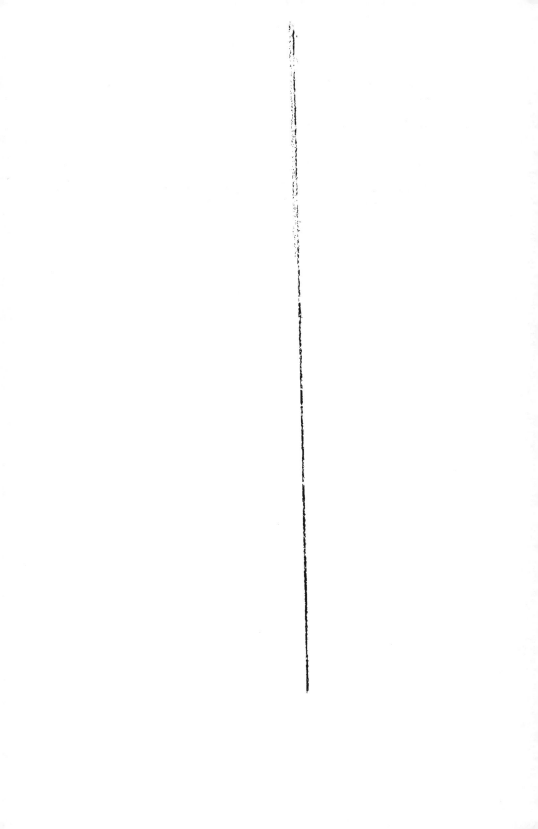

By the same Author.

1. FOUR LECTURES on the GROUNDS OF FAITH. 8vo, cloth,
   3s. 6d. ; by post, 4s.

2. A SERMON preached on the Feast of St. Ignatius. 1s.; by
   post, 1s. 4d.

3. A SERMON preached in the Synod of Oscott. 1s. ; by post, 1s. 4d.

4. THE LOVE OF JESUS OUR LAW : a Sermon in behalf of the
   Greenwich Catholic Schools. 1s. 6d. ; by post, 2s.

CPSIA information can be obtained
at www.ICGtesting.com
Printed in the USA
BVHW071620280119
538839BV00028B/2388/P